A Learning To Cook
ADIRONDACK
Over An Open Fire

Nancy P Best

Learning To Cook ADIRONDACK Over An Open Fire

Nancy Pulling Best

Learning To Cook ADIRONDACK *Over An Open Fire*

Nancy Pulling Best
Copyright © 2014

First Paperback Printing, July 2014

Published by
NDI Publishing
2985 Powell Road, Blossvale NY 13308
www.nancydidit.com

Printed in the United States of America
by Versa Press, Inc., Illinois

ISBN 978-0-9711638-4-3

Dedication

To Adirondackers
who are not afraid to cook
over an open fire.

Preface

After writing my first cook book, *Learning to Cook Adirondack*, I realized I have a number of friends and family members who consider the camp fire to be the original Adirondack kitchen.

In this edition, I have included stories, pictures and recipes of Adirondackers who love to cook over an open fire.

Nancy

Table of Contents

Gordy Rudd

Gordy Rudd grew up in Inlet, NY. He was the oldest of three sons born to Gordy and Inez Rudd who owned the Red & White grocery store. His grandfather, Dewy Rudd, ran the Coffee Cup Diner next door. I met Gordy in the fall of 1964, the beginning of 7th grade for Gordy and me.

For those of you who did not grow up in Inlet or Old Forge, the Inlet kids go to elementary school in Inlet and in 7th grade they continue at the Town of Webb Schools in Old Forge. Gordy and I were in the same grade right through graduation.

In the spring of 1970, we both went on a trip to England and Ireland with several kids from school. We toured London, spent some time in Bradford and then went to Ireland where we went to Glendalough, an Irish pub or two and of course the Guinness brewery.

After graduation we didn't see much of each other. I was in closer contact with

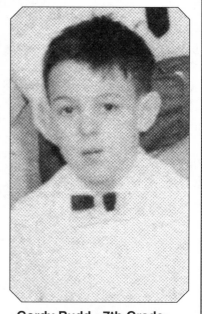

Gordy Rudd · 7th Grade

Gordy Rudd and Bob Spears in a taxi in London, England in 1970.

Gordy's youngest brother, Greg. Gordy read a copy of my first book, *Learning To Cook Adirondack*, and emailed me a comment. That comment inspired me to write this edition.

It seems Gordy has been a boy scout leader for a number of years. He brings his troop to the Adirondacks to camp out in all four seasons. He invited me to a cookout with his scout troop on his mom's front lawn on South Shore Road in Inlet.

When I arrived, I realized that these were some serious boy scouts. They came with canoes, tents, picnic tables, cupboards, chairs and a complete set up to cook everything from pancakes to pork roast.

Pork roast was on the menu that night complete with salad, mashed potatoes, gravy, vegetables and dessert... all prepared over an open fire. The roast was cooked in a trash can.

First Gordy took the roast and wrapped it in foil and chicken wire.

BSA Troop 711 of Hastings, NY traveled to Inlet in this truck for a cookout and camping trip in the fall of 2011.

He then hung it in the trash can and put the lid on. Three tubes were filled with charcoal and as the charcoal burned down, more was added. The roast cooked for two and a half to three hours. When the internal temperature was 165⁰, it was done.

Gordy says it works with almost any meat from beef to a turkey.

While the roast was cooking, Gordy made what he called a dump cake for dessert. He cooked it in a dutch oven right in the fire pit.

Gordy's friends like to refer to him as the "Emeril of the garbage can."

The boys were very well behaved and the dinner was one of the best I have ever had over an open fire.

When Gordy and I were in

The trash can had three tubes of chicken wire fixed to the sides and air holes cut near the bottom. The roast hung from a tripod.

DESSERT

Adirondack Recipe *Dump Cake*

1 can each:	cherry pie filling
whole berry cranberry sauce	raspberry pie filling
pineapple chunks	blackberry pie filling
mandarin oranges	Yellow cake mix

Drain pineapple & oranges. Mix all cans of fruit together in a foil lined cast iron dutch oven.

Make yellow cake mix as per directions on box. Pour batter over the fruit mixture.

Put dutch oven in hot coals. Arrange more coals on lid. Check frequently. Dessert is done when cake bounces back when touched.

Ireland, one night it was quite cold. Middle class homes in 1970s Ireland rarely had central heat. Usually there was only a small coal stove in the living room.

That night when Gordy retired his feet hit something warm in the bottom of his bed. After some investigation, he found that the lady of the house had placed a hot water bottle in the bed.

Several years later while camping on a very cold night, Gordy remembered the hot water bottle incident. He didn't

BSA Troop 711 of Hastings spread out on Inez Rudd's lawn for a late summer camp out.

11

have a hot water bottle so he put some warm water in a zip lock bag and put it in the bottom of his sleeping bag.

In the morning, when he got up he was about to empty the bag when one of the scouts saw him.

Gordy Rudd

"Hey, Mr. Rudd, were you too tired to get up and go to the out house last night?" the scout said.

At that, Gordy opened the bag and took a big sip. The whole troop was completely grossed out!

Gordy's motto is "When in doubt, improvise, overcome and adapt."

Good words to live by.

Scottie Best Glitz

If you grew up in the Adirondacks there are two things you knew. The first is how to get through a long, long winter and the second is how to get a summer job.

I worked all summer every summer from the time I was 12. My kids found themselves in the same situation.

Scottie and Kelly babysat and Jamie washed dishes for years. But finally they all wanted to get a "real" job. Scottie found her real job at the Pied Piper.

The Greene family owned the Pied Piper for most of my life. It was built in 1955 by the Sheehan family.

Kaisa Ahola, Kurt Gardner, Scottie Best and Stephanie Park worked together for years at the Pied Piper in Old Forge.

Al and Mary Greene arrived on the scene in 1956. Their oldest son, Albert, was in my grade. Their oldest daughter, Christine, was in my brother's grade and their son, Mike, was just a year behind Chris.

In the early 1990s, Mike took over running the Pied. Scottie worked for him for five years.

No matter where Scottie worked, she always ended up cooking or baking something delicious.

**Albert Greene
1962**

**Mike Greene
1964**

She learned to make ice cream cones, all kinds of sundaes, cole slaw and chili at the Pied.

That chili is perfect cooked over an open fire in a cast iron dutch oven. Scottie has had to cut the recipe down over the years. Now it serves a family not a 4th of July crowd.

 MAIN DISH

Adirondack Recipe *Pied Piper Chili*

2 - 2 1/2 lbs ground beef	1 - 2 tbsp chili powder
1 bag frozen pepper & onion strips	1/2 - 1 tsp crushed red pepper
28 oz can diced tomatoes, drained	1 tsp each salt & pepper
2 (15 oz) cans kidney beans	2 cups ketchup
(I use 1 dark & 1 light)	2 cups BBQ sauce*

In a large pot, brown ground beef with peppers and onions. Add tomatoes, beans and spices. Cook 5 to 10 minutes. Add ketchup and BBQ sauce. Simmer 15 to 20 minutes. Start with a small amount of spice. You can always add more but you can't take it out. Also, chili gets hotter the longer it cooks.

*BBQ sauce must be plain, original or the like. NO honey, sweet, brown sugar etc.

Johnny Evans

Once I decided to write *Learning To Cook Adirondack Over An Open Fire*, my brother, Bobby, insisted that I include one of his best friends. He claimed that Johnny Evans cooked the best camp food he ever tasted.

Bobby and Johnny were in kindergarten together. My mom, Betty Charbonneau Pulling, and Johnny's mom, Mary Burkhard Evans, were in the same grade, too.

Johnny started a business in the 1980s, Adirondack Saddle Tours. He has been riding horses for over 45 years and has been offering horseback riding in the Adirondack wilderness for over 25 years. He will take you on an hour ride or one so long that you need to stop for dinner. I only went horseback riding with Johnny once. My niece loved horses and wanted to go on a real ride. So

Town of Webb School Class of 1972 when Johnny and Bobby were in kindergarten. Front Row: Mike Ryan, C. Morse, L. Buckmiller, Donna Boudreau, Diane Winslow, Barb Decker, John Ball, Ricky Myers, John Codega. Middle: Terry Henderson, Annette Gaffney, Steve Ritz, Christine Greene, Ginny Winter, Millie Wark, Tom Clark, Timmy Leach, Ron Smith, Brad Newton, Danny VanAntwerp. Back: Johnny Evans, Chris Russell, Bobby Pulling, Bonnie LaFountain, Brenda Bemis, Mary Gregory, Kathleen Perkins, Maureen Perkins, Mike Pashley. (Names according to the 1960 Hadaronda yearbook. Courtesy of Randy Kokernot)

off we went to Eagle Bay and the most terrifying horseback ride I had ever been on. I retired my boots after that ride. But Johnny has gone on to give thousands of rides to happy Adirondack travelers.

About 26 years ago something happened to keep Johnny in the business. He started working with disabled folks. He told me that it changed everything.

"I promise you it's like magic," he said. "This one little girl always kept her head down and eyes closed. But when we put her up on her mom's lap on the horse... she picked her head up and opened her eyes."

Johnny has gone on to work with people with everything from autism, cerebral palsy and tourette's syndrome to PTSD.

He told me that he doesn't know what he cooked that my brother said was so good. Maybe it was the filet he marinaded and grilled or the turkey he smoked. He said there was a blueberry cobbler he used to make, too.

He couldn't remember what was in the marinade but he remembered one time they mixed up the amount of vinegar and the amount of oil and the meat just fell apart.

Johnny Evans

DESSERT

Adirondack Recipe	*Wild Blueberry Cobbler*

1 stick butter	1 tbsp baking powder
4 cups wild blueberries	1 tsp lemon juice
2 cups flour	1 tsp salt
1/2 cup sugar	2 tsp cinnamon
2 cups sugar	1 1/2 cups milk
1 tsp lemon zest	1/4 cup water

Melt butter in a 12" Dutch oven using 10-12 briquettes bottom heat. Wash fresh blueberries and drain. In a large bowl combine blueberries, 1/2 cup sugar, lemon zest, lemon juice, 1 tsp. of the cinnamon and water; stir to coat blueberries. Let rest. In a separate bowl combine flour, 2 cups sugar, baking powder, and salt; stir to mix. Add milk and beat until batter is smooth. Pour batter over melted butter, do not stir. Carefully spoon blueberries over top of the batter, do not stir. Sprinkle remaining cinnamon over the top. Cover and bake using 10-12 briquettes bottom and 18-20 briquettes top for 45 to 60 minutes rotating oven and lid 1/4 turn in opposite directions every 10 minutes until crust is golden brown. Serve topped with whipped cream or serve with vanilla ice cream. Serves: 10

Jay O'Hern & Noah John Rondeau

I moved to the Camden, NY area in 1996. I owned a weekly newspaper there and met author Jay O'Hern. Jay and his wife, Betty, were teachers in the Camden School district and at least one of my grandchildren was lucky enough to have them as a teacher.

Jay started camping in the Adirondacks when he was four years old and he has spent time in the Adirondacks every year since that time. He loves to hike and has more information in his head about the mountains than I do... and I grew up there.

William "Jay" O'Hern

He has written several books including *Life with Noah, Noah John Rondeau's Wilderness Days, The Hermit and Us* and *Adirondack Wilds*.

He became interested in the Adirondack Hermit in 1969 after reading Maitland DeSormo's book, *Noah John Rondeau: Adirondack Hermit.*

Jay met Rich Smith, one of Noah's best friends, through DeSormo. Smith spent 25 years with Noah and 10 years in a cabin six miles above Noah. Jay was able to learn a great deal about the life and habits of Noah from him.

Being an Adirondack Hermit led Noah to cook over an open fire more than the average man. I wanted to include at least a couple of Noah's recipes in this book. He refered to his cooking as "Exotic Backwoods Cookery."

MAIN DISH

Adirondack Recipe <u>*Onion Venison Slam Bang Stew*</u>

Take a piece of venison about the size of two good goose eggs. Fry it out in a kettle and when nearly done add five onions. Fry until brown and almost done, then add six potatoes, sliced and enough water to cover. Cook until potatoes are done, then add a pint of canned milk diluted with water. When this comes to the boiling point take it off the fire and add salt and pepper.

 MAIN DISH

Adirondack Recipe <u>*Poverty Casserole*</u>

The casserole consists of anything considered edible actually (within reason). In a deep pan lined with jellied cornmeal mush, add layers of wild meat. Whatever scraps you have around: rabbit, beaver, grouse, squirrel. To those layers add thin spreadings of sourdough pancake batter. You can even add potato parings. Sprinkle with raisins and beechnuts. Bake until golden brown.

This turned out to be a backwoods delicacy. Noah often ate it along the trap line and found it served as an energy booster that was guaranteed to quicken his pace on snowshoes.

Noah scratched this next recipe across the back of a Morning Glory evaporated milk label he handed to Richard Smith.

Noah John Rondeau

 MAIN DISH

Adirondack Recipe _The Best Tasting Rock Ever_

Take a large pot and bring a gallon and a half of water to a boil. While it's reaching the boiling point, find a rock about half the size of a merganser duck. Add the rock and the duck to the pot. After a half hour's boil, a black scum will rise to the top. Remove the scum with a wooden spoon. Don't for any reason use a metal utensil. It will disintegrate. When the scum ceases to rise, the duck should have turned black. Don't be alarmed. This only indicates it is cooked and time to test the contents. Stick a fork in the rock. If you can do this, throw the duck away and eat the rock.

Later, Richard Smith began experimenting with dehydrated ingredients. They were lightweight and were packed with nourishment. On one of his many trips to the hermitage he brought a large package that guaranteed it would serve two people. Noah promised he would try it out at a later date. A few months later Smith noted Rondeau had penned "Smith's Favorite Vegetable Soup" on a sheet of paper. It was tacked on a pole inside the wigwam where Noah knew Richard would eventually see it posted. Noah had crossed out serving for two and written "eight or more hungry mountain climbers."

The formula was simple. Add the contents of Richard's dehydrated vegetable mix to a quart of boiling water. If more company arrives drop in more beans and a pail of water. It was his way of being funny.

I wanted to include a recipe for stew made with wild meat. My daughter, Scottie, makes great venison stew but you can use any meat in her recipe.

Jay O'Hern wanted me to remind you about some of those meats. Remember another name for woodchuck is groundhog. This wild game meat is a tried and true food and not just at fish and game club dinners. You can grind it for patties, stew and fry the meat, make groundhog pie, fricassee, and hide the meat in tomato sauce.

He wanted me to make sure to mention the preparation should follow the same general rules for handling any wild meat – like the blood should be drained, and the entrails removed and the body cavity wiped and washed clean.

I'm told that when a woodchuck is hung in a cooler for 48 hours, it is ready to be skinned and cooked.

The meat is dark, but mild flavored and tender. It does not require soaking; however, many people like to soak it overnight in salt water. If the woodchuck is caught just before she begins her winter sleep, there is an insulating fat layer under the skin. Remove excess fat and the seven to nine scent glands or "kernels" some call them in the small of the back and under the forearms. It's recommended to parboil the meat of older animals. It's standard practice to cook the meat using recipes that call for chicken or rabbit. Jay's wife would never even consider him using one of her pots or crock pot. He prefers to hide the taste of wild meat by using tomato sauce in the recipe.

Noah John Rondeau

MAIN DISH

Adirondack Recipe — *Wild Meat Stew*

2 lbs meat	1 large onion
2 cups red wine	4-5 ribs celery
1 quart beef broth	1-2 lbs potatoes
1 packet pot roast seasoning	8 oz sliced mushrooms
	2-4 tbsp flour
1 lb carrots	salt and pepper to taste

Cut meat in one inch cubes. Brown meat with 2 tbsp oil in dutch oven. Cover with the wine, pot roast seasoning, and 2 cups beef broth. Cook over low heat for 1 hour. Chop onion, carrots, and celery, add to pot along with remaining broth (reserve 1/2 cup broth). Cook another 30 minutes. Chop potatoes, add to pot with mushrooms. Cook another 20 minutes. Stir together flour and reserved broth to make a slurry, making sure there are no lumps. Add slurry to stew stirring briskly. Cook for about 10 minutes, add salt and pepper to taste.

I was looking for a Blueberry Duffs recipe and mentioned it to Jay. He had access to recipes that were prepared at Camp Cozy at North Lake. Camp Cozy was there from about 1887 to the later 1930s. The Adirondack League Club drove everyone out of the camp when they leased the property from the Gould Paper Company.

DESSERT

Adirondack Recipe   _Blueberry Duffs_

2 tbsp sugar	2 tsp Baking Powder
1/2 cup butter	1 1/2 cups flour
1/2 cup milk	1 cup blueberries
1 egg	
Put in buttered cups and steam 1/2 hour	

Sabrina Gribneau Nedell

The Gribneaus are another family that is intertwined with mine. The family homestead is on 6th Lake in Inlet. I graduated from high school with Ginny and my girls went to school with Sabrina. They all learned how to cross country ski when they went to elementary school in Inlet.

Back in the day, all of the Inlet Common School children skied with Walter Schmid every winter. The Inlet school didn't have a gym so they had to be creative with their Physical Education.

Sabrina is now married and living on the north shore of Oneida Lake in Jewell, NY. Several of my grandchildren and Sabrina's children all go to school in Camden, NY.

Sabrina and I are friends on Facebook. I am also her friend on her Adk Girl page which shows off her pottery. Recently I was the winner of a drawing she offered. I am now the proud owner of an igloo and three snowmen that she made.

Sabrina Gribneau Nedell

One day as I was looking around Facebook, I saw that Sabrina had an interesting post call *Cooking On A Log*. It also said "Please post." So here it is.

Cut the log evenly on both sides so it stands up freely. Then cut it into vertical segments most of the way down the length of the log. Stuff some newspaper into the cracks as deep as you can get it, leaving a wick at the bottom, and light it up. That's all there is to it – the log burns from the inside out, and you have a simple, handmade stove.

I thought it was an excellent idea and a quick way to make yourself an outdoor cooker.

by Adk Girl aka Sabrina

Greg Rudd

I have known Greg Rudd since I was a child. He and his two brothers, Gordy and Gary, grew up in Inlet, but I really got to know him well when we both attended the Inlet Community Church.

He is a teacher, a potter and he loves to hunt. His idea of a great weekend is to go back into his hunting camp just outside of Big Moose with a bunch of the guys and hunt deer.

His grandfather, Dewey Rudd, built the original camp in 1939. Before that he built one back in the Moose River Plains on state land. The forest ranger told him to rip it down or he would burn it down. Dewey didn't so the forest ranger did.

Dewey and his son Gordy, Sr. hunted at the camp in Big Moose for about 20 years before they sold it in the late 1950s. For

Greg Rudd

the last 20 years, Greg and his brother Gordy, Jr., have been part of a group which has the rights to the camp and about 2500 acres of good land to hunt on.

Each year when they get their first deer the tradition is to have what Greg calls a Venison Fry. It all happens on the top of a wood stove in the camp. Dewey had a frying pan made that is just the size of the top of the stove. It is about two by

The original hunting camp Dewey Rudd built back in 1939

three feet. First you get the pan really hot, about 600^0. Greg says you can tell when the pan is hot enough as the stove pipe will glow cherry red. Then you throw about a half pound of butter, two diced white onions, two diced green peppers and about ten pounds of a hind quarter that has been cubed into the hot pan. Now according to Greg you have to take off all the fat and silver meat (which includes the tendons). Then you stir all the ingredients in the pan at once. In about five minutes the dish is done.

The trick is that you have to get the meat out of the pan so it doesn't keep cooking. Add to that some potatoes, veggies and maybe a salad and you can feed around 15 hungry men.

Back in the mid-1980s, Greg's mother, Inez Rudd, let me taste the hind quarter of a beaver she had roasted. I have never forgotten the taste and texture of that roast. It may have been the best meat I have ever tasted. Greg was good enough to share the recipe with me and now with you.

Dewey, from left, Evelyn, Gordy and Mildred Rudd at the Red & White Grocery in Inlet, NY.

MAIN DISH

Adirondack Recipe   _Venison Roast_

Hind Quarter Venison Roast   several sliced carrots
1 lb Salt Pork in strips   and a couple sliced onions
1 pkg dry onion soup mix

When you cut up the deer, bone out the hind quarter.
Take out all the silver meat and tendons. While the
meat is laid out, put 1/2 pound of the salt pork on the
meat. Tie up the roast. Then put the other 1/2 pound
of strips on the top of the roast and tie it there.
Put the roast in a lisk roaster (turkey pan) with half
and inch of water in the bottom. Surround with onion
and carrot slices and sprinkle soup mix on top. Cover
and cook 6 to 7 hours at 275° or until it reaches an
internal temperature between 135° and 140°·

 MAIN DISH

Adirondack Recipe   _Roast Beaver_

Beaver Carcass   salt
1 pkg dry onion soup mix   2 onions

Clean and de-gland the carcass, take out all fat.
Soak in salt water over night. Drain and pat dry.
Roast slow for 6 hours at 275° in a covered pan sealed
tight with 2 onions cut up and a package of dry onion
soup mix sprinkled over it.
It is a fine textured red meat like venison.

Katie Niedzlieski Best

My daughters graduated from the Town of Webb High School in Old Forge. By the time my son got ready to graduate I had taken a job in Holland Patent so he graduated as a Golden Night. His best friend during his high school years continues to be his best friend as well as his cousin-in-law... if there is such a thing.

Jamie & Katie Best

Jamie married Katie Niedzlieski, a young lady who turned out to be just perfect for him. She is an athlete just like he is. She played field hockey in high school and college. She loves sports and understands them just like he does.

Another thing I love about Katie is that she loves the mountains just like he does.

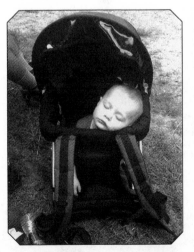

Nathan after his first climb.

Katie's family did a lot of camping when she was growing up. Her parents have a camp on the Black River and they spend as much time up there as they can. It really is a true camp... no indoor plumbing.

The summer after their son, Nathan, was born they climbed Blue Mountain and Rocky Mountain with him in a pack on Jamie's back. The hope is that he and his brother, Matthew, will learn to love the mountains and camping as much as their parents.

Katie remembers cooking "Dough Boys" over the open fire as a kid. It is a treat that can be used as breakfast or a dessert.

You take dough and put it on the end of a stick. Then you cook it over the fire like you do a marshmallow.

The trick is that you need a fat stick. When the dough is cooked you pull the stick out and fill the hole with jam. The dough that Katie's mom used was pizza dough, the kind you get in a bag in the refrigerator section in the grocery store. You can also use refrigerator biscuit dough or crescent roll dough.

The perfectly cook Dough Boy.

I found that the pizza dough works the best. It is easy to handle even when it warms up. It cooks up firm and leaves a nice hole when taken off the stick. The crescent roll dough tastes the best, probably because it has so much butter in it. The dough is hard to handel if it gets warm and when it is cooked is a softer product. The biscuit dough is okay. It tastes good and is hard to work with when it warms up. Of the three, it is my third choice.

Cooking dough on a stick is tricky. It is a lot like cooking marshmallows. If you get too close to the fire, it burns on the outside and is raw on the inside. You need some nice coals and patience. You

Kaisa and Katie cooking dough over an open fire,

need to turn the stick and turn the stick and turn the stick to make sure it cooks evenly. It might take a time or two to get it right. But when you do I guarantee you will love the product.

My granddaughter, Kaisa, thinks you should fill the hole with jam for breakfast, peanut butter for lunch and melted chocolate for dessert. She would eat them all day long.

🌲 **MAIN DISH**

Adirondack Recipe   *Cheeseburger Dough Boy*

1 lb ground beef	1/4 cup relish
1/4 cup diced onion	1 cup shredded cheese
1/4 cup ketchup	

Brown beef and onion. Add ketchup relish and cheese.
Spoon mixture into do-boys.
Tastes just like a cheeseburger.

Girls Scouts

Several generations of my family grew up in the Adirondacks. Sometimes there is so much to do, you couldn't do it all if you wanted to. But sometimes there is almost nothing to do. I learned to take advantage of everything there was to do in the off season and I taught my kids to do the same thing.

One of those things was Girl Scouts. I was a scout as long as there was a troop for me to join. My daughters were scouts, too. When they were scouts I was a leader and cookie mother.

Scouting taught me to cook over an open fire, sometimes in a pan and sometimes right in the fire.

My brother-in-law, Mike, had a troop of Royal Ambassadors, those are like scouts in the Baptist church. He used to take them camping all the time. One time he had the fire going good. He told the boys to wrap their potatoes in foil and put them in the fire. He then took the boys for a hike. The fire was very hot and when they got back the potatoes, foil and all, were completely burned up. Mike warns not to leave potatoes in too hot a fire for too long!

Scottie & Kelly Best at a Girl Scout Jamboree

My girls remember cooking lots of things in foil in the fire. Here are a few.

 MAIN DISH

Adirondack Recipe   _Hobo Dinner_

Ground beef or turkey	_Diced carrot_
Diced onion	_Diced potato_

Put vegetables in heavy-duty foil. Put meat on top of vegetables. Wrap foil tight. Place directly on hot coals. Cook 30 to 45 minutes until meat is done. Salt and pepper to taste.

SIDE DISH

Adirondack Recipe   *Campfire Baked Potatoes*

One potato for each person

Scrub each potato well and poke several times with a fork. Wrap each potato separately in aluminum foil. Double wrap even if you are using heavy-duty foil. Place foil-wrapped potatoes directly on the hot coals and embers of your fire.

Cook potatoes for 45 minutes or until you can poke potatoes with a fork easily.

 DESSERT

Adirondack Recipe   *Campfire Baked Bananas*

One banana for each person   marshmallows

chocolate chips   berries

peanut butter   candy pieces

Pull back one section of banana peel. Make a cut into banana about half way through, lengthwise. Fill banana with any combination of chocolate chips, marshmallows, peanut butter, peanut butter cups, berries, or candy bar pieces. Replace peel and wrap banana in foil. Place banana in hot coals for about 5 minutes.

The one thing that everybody knows about girl scouts is that they make s'mores. Between my daughters and daughter-in-law they have come up with some unique s'mores. Now the regular recipe is two graham crackers with a square of chocolate and a perfectly toasted marshmallow.

Katie likes to make s'mores with a peanut butter cup instead of just milk chocolate. She also says a brownie in place of the graham crackers is good but it is so rich you almost can't eat it.

Another variation is to make the original recipe and add slices of bananas or strawberries just before the warm marshmallow.

Maybe you want to try it another way all together.

DESSERT

Adirondack Recipe   *No Mess S'mores*

tortillas   mini-marshmallows

chocolate

Take a tortilla and lay it in a pan or anything over the fire until it's warm. Once the tortilla's warm, add chocolate and mini-marshmallows and roll up.

MAIN DISH

Adirondack Recipe   *Bacon & Onion Packet Potatoes*

3 sheets heavy duty foil	*1 sm. onion thinly sliced*
1 pkg onion soup mix	*1 cup grated cheese*
10-12 baby red potatoes	*salt & pepper to taste*
thinly sliced	*3 tbsp butter*
12 slices cooked bacon	

Spray each sheet of foil with cooking spray. Top each sheet with equal portions of sliced potatoes, bacon, soup mix, onions and cheese (optional). Salt and pepper to taste. Top each one with a tablespoon of butter. Wrap securely. Grill for 20 to 30 minutes or until potatoes are cooked. Let stand 10 minutes before serving.

Mark Hudon

In the early 1980s, I lived in Thendara. My family became good friends with Carol and Steve Franks and their children. We both had three kids and together we had three boys and three girls.

After a long winter and disappointing spring the sun finally came out. It was a prefectly beautiful day and Carol and I wanted to have a cook out. So we searched our refrigerators and the best we could come up with was the makings for tacos. I had never thought of cooking tacos over an open fire but was willing to give it a try.

We diced, chopped and shredded what we needed and set out for Lock-n-dam. We cooked the ground beef over a fire in a large cast iron frying pan and warmed the shells by hanging them on sticks over the fire. We were just starting to assemble the tacos when a young man dressed all in his red plaid hunting clothes and waders arrived on the other side of the river.

He turned out to be Mark Hudon and he strolled out across the dam into the water and started fishing. I was concerned because the Moose River was high, the spring melt off was cold and I knew how slippery the dam could be. We continued eating and Mark continued fishing. The kids were running around having a great time.

All of a sudden Mark went down. We all jumped up in a panic. He was under water for what seemed to be too long. Just then he popped up for a breath of air. It occurred to me that his waders were full of water and he was

Scottie Best, back, Kelly Best, Melinda Franks, front, Jamie Best, Chris Franks and Steve Franks.

probably trying to get them off. Our husbands were in full panic mode and ready to jump in the river with Mark. I suggested that they not jump in the rushing, ice cold water but rather get some rope or a long stick and try to help Mark get out of the river.

While we were trying to figure out how to help, Mark got his waders off and the water washed him far enough down stream so he could reach the shore and pull himself out. He was embarrassed but I was so happy to see him on dry land.

He only had one thing to say, "Please don't tell my dad. He'll kill me."

Mark Hudon

MAIN DISH

Adirondack Recipe   _Adirondack Tacos_

2 lbs ground beef	2 cups diced tomatoes
2 pkgs taco seasoning	24 taco shells
2 cups shredded cheese	Optional: diced onions,
2 cups shredded lettuce	black olives, refried beans

Over a hot fire, cook ground beef in cast iron frying pan. Add taco seasoning and 1 cup water. Stir and simmer 4 minutes. Warm shells by hanging them on sticks and holding them over the fire. Assemble tacos and enjoy in the great outdoors.

Jerry & Maggie Ernenwein

Jerry Ernenwein was my older brother's best friend. Jerry graduated from high school and then came to Old Forge and did a year of post graduate work at the Town of Webb. He had worked summers at Camp Monroe on 4th Lake and he just loved the Adirondacks. He found himself in my brother Pepper's grade and they became fast friends.

Jerry Ernenwein

The first time he came to dinner at our house I remember we had salad with the meal. We always had Miracle French dressing. It was by Kraft and was quite oily. It had to be shaken up before every use. Jerry asked for the dressing to be passed to him. When he shook it, the top was not on tight and the dressing went all over his shirt.

Maggie Tobin (that was her maiden name) was my sister's roommate at SUNY Brockport. The first time Maggie came to visit, my mom was out in front of her store weeding her flower garden. My sister, Peggy, pulled up in her Volkswagen Beetle and the two of them got out of the car. My mother started walking towards them and stepped on the nozzle end of the hose. It was the kind that sprayed water when you squeezed the handle. Mom stepped on it and it sprayed water right up her dress hitting her in the face. She was so surprised she didn't take her foot off the hose. She was mad but it sure was funny.

Maggie and Jerry got married a couple of years later. She had twins girls and I had twin girls the same year. She had a son the same age as my son Jamie but then I got out of the race. She ended up with six, three boys and three girls.

We raised our kids together in Inlet for several years. Her kids called my mother Grandma Betty. We were like family. One time when Maggie and I were on a Girl Scout outing at the Enchanted Forest, several of the scouts wanted to ride the Salt-N-Pepper Shakers. I had ridden one at the Boonville Fair several years earlier with my sister, Peggy. I was so scared that I promised God if He got me off that ride I would never go on it again. I was not about to break my promise to God for some Girl Scouts.

Finally Maggie relented and got on the ride with the brave scouts. She had brought her youngest son, David, with her on the outing. David was allergic to almost everything. He was on a very strict diet. As the ride started Maggie shouted out the window, "If anything happens to me, don't feed David anything!"

As luck would have it, when the ride stopped, Maggie disembarked and everything went back to normal.

Maggie remembers making "buddy burners" in Girl Scouts. She said you took a tuna can, coiled corrugated cardboard tightly in the can. The cardboard needed to be a little taller than the can. Then you poured wax on the cardboard. Over that you put a three pound coffee can with some vents cut in it. You would light the cardboard put the coffee can inverted over the tuna can and you had yourself a outdoor cook stove.

Luke Ernenwein, from left, Ginny Ernenwein, Kelly Best, Scottie Best and Kathy Ernenwein making candy house for Christmas in Inlet around 1981.

MAIN DISH

Adirondack Recipe _Campfire Stew_

1 lb ground beef	2 cans vegetable soup
chopped onions and peppers	2 cups cooked
2 cans tomato soup	elbow maccaroni

Soap the outside of your pan first. It will be easier to clean. Over a hot fire, cook ground beef, onions and peppers. Stir in maccaroni and cans of soup. Heat until bubbling.

The Flying Wallendas

I grew up with the Enchanted Forest. I can't remember a time when it was not there. It was built in 1956, I was four years old. Almost everyone who lives or lived in the area knew the Wallendas, maybe not personally but at least by reputation. I was luckier than most. I know them as good friends.

The year I met my husband he was working at the Forest. The Wallendas were working there, too. We became great friends with Tino.

A few years later, Tino returned with his wife, Olinka, and baby daughter, Alida. I had twin girls and we all spent a lot of time together. We have stayed friends over the years.

Whenever they are anywhere near us we go see them perform. They came to our church in Chicago, New Hartford, Inlet, and to the lake

Luis Murillo, Karl Wallenda and Tino Wallenda

front at Sylvan Beach and put on shows... just because we asked them to.

When we lived in Chicago, our girls were in kindergarten. They wanted to bring our 8 x 10 publicity photo of Tino and Olinka to school for show and tell. I let them but told them not to lose it or there would be trouble. They were late coming home that day. Just as I was about to start worrying the phone rang. It was the principal, she explained that they had looked all over the school and couldn't find the picture anywhere. The girls told her they couldn't go home without that picture and the principal begged me to let them come home. I was a little embarrassed and assured her they were welcome to come home. When I told Tino the story he sent a new autographed picture in full color.

I have had the pleasure of watching the Wallenda children grow up. Now to be fair there are no Wallenda children... at least not born with that last name. Karl only had two daughters who reproduced. Tino's name at birth was Alberto Giovanni Zoppe. His family started calling him Albertino and it got shortened to Tino. At one point he changed his name to Tino Wallenda Zoppe. So when he had kids he picked first names with an A so their initials would be A. Z.

Tino's wife, Olinka, is a great cook. I asked her for a recipe for her apple strudel once. When I got it, it was about nine pages long. When she makes something from scratch... it is from scratch.

Tino's oldest daughter, Alida, is married to a flying trapeze artist. So now she not only walks the high wire but flies through the air with the greatest of ease. She spends a lot of time in the summer at the Enchanted Forest when she is not at the Big Apple Circus.

Ysabella, Alida's oldest daughter, works with her mom and dad's act. Last year I watched her on Good Morning America as she tried to teach one of the hosts to fly. She is only 10 but she's already so grown up.

Andrea is retired from the troup. She is a full time mom now. Aurelia and Alex are still working with Tino. Olinka is no longer on the wire but she is still a big part of the act. Somebody has to keep them all organized! They do so many different acts sometimes they put on a circus all by themselves.

Tino, Alida, Alex, Andrea, Aurelia and Olinka Wallenda

SIDE DISH

Adirondack Recipe _Cucumber Salad_

large cucumber grated	_1/4 cup mayonnaise_
green onion sliced	_1/4 red wine vinegar_
Fresh dill chopped	_Salt to taste_
1/4 cup sour cream	

Mix all ingredients. Chill.

Alida told me she never measures. She does every-thing by eye. The measurements are mine. Feel free to add or subtract as you see fit.

Tino & Olinka on the high wire. This is the replacement photo they sent my girls.

Florence Eleilia Jones Preston

I have made some of my best friends going to church. It is a great place to meet people. One day when I was working at a medium sized church as the children's director, the phone rang. It was a young mother, Eleilia, who was profoundly pregnant and already had two small children. She was attending another church in the area. Her husband was in the service and found himself working many Sunday mornings. She needed help getting herself and the two small children into the church building and asked if someone in our church would help her as no one at her church would. I told her that I would be happy to help her and we have been friends ever since.

Scott & Eleilia Preston

Her kids call me Grandma Nancy. One winter I traveled to her home town in West Virginia with Eleilia and her kids. She is from Lewisburg, WV. It reminded me of my beautiful Adirondacks. The mountains are just breath taking. The difference is that her mountains come down to fields with grazing cattle and the Adirondacks come down to forests and more mountains.

While I was in West Virginia it snowed. I don't mean an inch or two. It really snowed. They all blamed me for bringing it down with me. I have to tell you, those mountains looked even better with snow on them!

When Eleilia heard I was planning a cookbook about cooking over an open fire, she wanted to include her pudding recipe. It began

Florence & Cohen Jones

with her great grandmother, Florence Bostic, who shared it with her daughter-in-law, Nina Jane Bostic, who shared it with her daughter, Florence Jones. Who shared it with her daughter, Florence Jones Preston but we call her Eleilia.

The original Florence cooked it over an open fire. Now Eleilia can make it in the microwave but she says it is easier on the gas stove... and that's kind of like an open fire!

Nina Jane Bostic

Florence Bostic

DESSERT

Adirondack Recipe   _Chocolate Pudding_

| 3/4 cup sugar | 3 tbsp cocoa |
| 1/2 cup flour | 2 cups milk |

Combine sugar, flour and cocoa. Add milk and cook in microwave (or over an open fire) 2 1/2 minutes stir, and continue cooking and stirring every 1 to 2 minutes until thickened.

My Mountaineer grandkids, Megan, Michael and Annabell.

Fish Stories

Paul & Christian Glitz

I have been very blessed all my life. Two of those blessings are my son-in-law, Paul, and his son, Christian. My daughter, Scottie, met Paul working at the Adirondack Buffet. If you have been around Old Forge for as long as I have been you will know it as Howard Johnson's even though it hasn't been that for years. When Paul was first introduced to Scottie, she was told his nickname was Scope. When she asked why, Paul said, "Because my kisses are minty fresh."

Paul loves to go camping, fishing and swimming. He was raised in Florida. The first time his dad took him fishing he was standing on a sea wall. His dad went to get the tackle box and Paul got a hit. The fish was pulling him and he

Paul & Scottie Glitz

Paul, Sr., Paul, Jr. and Paula Glitz

yelled for his father. Paul, Sr. looked up and said, "You better not drop that pole."

It turned out Paul, Jr. had caught a sting ray but lucky for him, he did not drop the pole.

Paul is not a cook at all but I had to include his recipe for cooking steak over the open fire. Get the pan rocket hot and let the steak cook 18 seconds on each side. He would eat it raw if it were socially acceptable.

Scottie is the cook of the family and I have included

several of her recipes in this book. Paul catches it or shoots it and Scottie cooks it. It is a marriage made in heaven.

Christian is his mom and dad's middle child. When he was tiny they moved to Fort Campbell, KY. Paul was in the Army. We didn't get to see too much of him when he was little. The whole family came to New York to see us for a few days. When they got ready to leave, I asked if the kids could stay and we would bring them home in a few days.

Paul and Scottie said yes and got in the car and drove away. I looked at that little guy who hardly knew us and expected him to start crying. He didn't and he never asked where his mom and dad were. That shows you just how much fun it is to be at Grandma and Grandpa's house!

Christian wanted me to print his favorite open fire recipe.

Christian Glitz

 ### DESSERT

Adirondack Recipe   *Baked Apples*

1 apple for each person   butter

brown sugar   cinnamon

Cut apple in half. Spread butter and brown sugar on apple. Sprinkle with cinnamon. Put two halfs back together and wrap in heavy duty aluminum foil. Put in hot coals. After 15 minutes, apple is done if knife slides in easily. Options include lemon juice, raisins, chopped walnuts and maple syrup.

Bernita Powers

One Sunday morning in church, in the dead of winter, we had a visitor. If you have ever gone to church in the winter in Inlet you know that is unusual. Right away my friend, Carol, and I introduced ourselves to the visitor. It was an older lady who was living at Camp Gorham for the winter. Her name was Bernita Powers and she had a camp on Twitchell Lake that was not winterized. So she found herself at Camp Gorham for the winter.

Bernita Powers

Carol and I decided to visit her during the week. Bernita offered us tea and we accepted. When the tea came, I put sugar and milk in mine. The milk curdled. Carol tasted hers and made a face. We pretended that we had finished our tea and took the cups to the sink. We had a very nice visit and after awhile we left.

When we got in the car, we were so upset. This poor woman had no winterized home and the winter home she found had undrinkable water. We were on the verge of tears not knowing what to do for her.

The very next Sunday Bernita came to church again. She made a beeline for Carol and me. She apologized over and over. It seems she had forgotten she had been cleaning her tea kettle with vinegar. Since she had coffee on our visit, she didn't know until much later that she had made our tea with boiling vinegar.

We became the best of friends and spent lots of time together for several years. We often talked about our first visit.

Back in those days, we ate together every Wednesday night at church. It was a weekly pot luck dinner and we had to be creative not to have the same dinners week after week.

One week Bernita brought fried perch. She loved to fish and had gotten quite a catch in the early spring. Some of the pieces of fish looked strange. Upon asking, she told me that she also fried the roe, egg sack. I must have made a face. She assured me that the fried roe tasted just like the fish and you could feed it to small children and not have to worry about any bones.

The Knoll cottage built in 1923 by Earl Covey on Twitchell Lake. Bernita and her husband bought it in the late 1950s

 MAIN DISH

Adirondack Recipe   Pan Fried Perch

Fresh Perch & roe	butter
salt & pepper	milk
flour	egg

Clean fish. Put some flour in a shallow dish. Sprinkle with salt and pepper. Mix milk and egg in shallow dish. Dip fish in milk mixture, dredge in flour mixture. Melt butter in cast iron frying pan until bubbling. Fry fish 5 minutes on each side until golden brown. Carefully add the roe to the pan and cook on the first side for two to three minutes, until golden brown. Turn and cook for 2 to 3 more minutes. Cover the pan and cook all for 3 to 4 minutes, until cooked through.

Ronnie Lyon

The first person I ever knew with hyper activity was Ronnie Lyon. I met him when my family moved back to the Adirondacks from Chicago. He was a teenager who lived in Inlet and went to church with me.

One day Ronnie and I were sitting in the church reading the Bible together. He looked up at me and said, "Nancy, how old are you, 40 what?"

I almost fell over, I was 28 at the time! I wasn't ever sure if he was fooling around or being serious.

He loved to hunt and fish. One day he caught two very big lake trout. He asked me to cook them. I was happy to comply and my whole family enjoyed a wonderful fish dinner.

Ronnie took the bones

Ronnie Lyon

out to my garbage can and we sat down to enjoy a movie. Shortly I heard a commotion in my garage. I just knew that my cats, I had three, were trying to get the fish bones out of the garbage. I went out the door clapping my hands and shouting at the cats to leave the bones alone.

What I encountered were three of the biggest racoons I have ever seen. Needless to say, I let the coons have the bones and I ran back inside.

Several nights later, Ronnie came into the house all excited. It seems there was a racoon up in the tree outside my house. My husband and Ronnie ran out to see if they could "catch" it. I was not sure what they had in mind. Ronnie got his bow and while my husband held the flashlight, Ronnie shot up into the tree. All he accomplished was pinning the coon to the tree by shooting him through the tail. Not giving it a second thought, Ronnie climbed up the tree and pulled the arrow out of the coon. Luck must have been on his side. The coon ran.

Ronnie not only brought me fish but also ducks and venison. He was the most helpful young man I ever met. If I needed something done, all I had to do was ask, give him a candy bar and a soda and he would work all day.

The thing I loved the most about Ronnie was the fact that he was so full of life. It was never quiet when he was around.

Ronnie Lyon

🌲 MAIN DISH

Adirondack Recipe *Lake Trout*

Fresh Lake Trout (4 lbs)	lemons
salt	onions
pepper	butter

Clean fish. Spread butter, the size of the fish, on heavy duty aluminum foil. Lay fish on butter, opened up. Inside fish, lay several slices of lemon and onion. Sprinkle with salt and pepper. Close fish and wrap in foil tightly so the butter doesn't run out. Place in a pan or on a grill over a low fire, you should hear the butter boiling. Cook for 40 minutes flipping the trout every ten minutes.

Gary & Karen Lee

Gary and Karen Lee came to Inlet in 1966. They came from the West Canada area where Gary was the last to serve there as a Forest Ranger. It was a remote area which presented many challenges and with one baby the first year and two the second, one challenge was doing the laundry. They had no electricity and no running water.

Karen got lots of exercise scrubbing diapers on a washboard in a tub just outside the front door of their cabin. When Karen heard there was a job available in Inlet and the cabin had a road right outside the front door... she started packing!

Gary and Karen were next door neighbors back in the Balston Spa area growing up. I heard a story

Erin Lee in a 1965 baby bath tub.

that Gary took Karen fishing early one April when they were just kids. As the story goes, it was so cold out that Gary had to keep the worms in his mouth to keep them from freezing.

Gary was a little ahead of Karen in school and when they were in high school they didn't run with the same crowd. But in the spring of 1963 he went over to her house and borrowed her typewriter from her mother so he could write some resumes. When Karen got home and he brought the typewriter back, the sparks flew. Good sparks... they were married the same year.

Although they moved to the area while I was still in high school, I didn't meet them until the early 1980s.

Karen and I both worked with ACT Inc. and the Inlet Players putting on productions all through the 1980s. We both worked back stage but sometimes Karen got right out on stage. She is one very funny lady, especially when she teams up with Terry Lehnen.

Gary is a noted birdwatcher, photographer and writer. He has written a column in the Adirondack Express for over 25 years. In his spare time he still likes to fish and there is nothing better when you are fishing than fresh caught fish cooked right then and there. For such occasions, Gary makes his famous "fish on a stick."

Karen & Gary Lee in 1965

MAIN DISH

Adirondack Recipe *Fish-on-a-Stick*

One Fish	salt & pepper to taste
(legal size trout is best)	One stick

Catch legal size trout. Clean fish. Take stick and sharpen one end. Starting at tail end, weave stick through fish so it will not fall off during cooking process. Make fire. When you have some nice coals, hold fish over coals until done. Time depends on size of fish and fire. About 10 minutes. Serve with salt and pepper.

Bill Pulling

From the time I was old enough to hold a fishing pole... I did. A bunch of us used to go down a short road next to DeCamps in Thendara when I was a kid and fish for bullheads in the Moose River.

First we would go over to the third green of the Thendara Golf Course and pick night crawlers and the next morning we would go fishing.

Sometimes my father, Bill Pulling, would take my brothers, sisters and me fishing on First Lake. He always told us he had permission to fish off the dock but we didn't care, we just liked to fish.

On one trip to the lake, my father had just gotten a new rod and reel. My older sister, Peggy, wanted to try it out. She begged and begged and finally Dad relented and let her try.

He took great care to show her how to cast. It seems you had to press down with your thumb on a button, put the

The Pullings in 1958, back, Betty, Edie, Bill; middle, Nancy, Peggy, Pepper and Bobby in the front.

rod back and when you cast the line you had to let your thumb off the button. She did it almost perfectly, except when she took her thumb off the button, she let go and threw the rod and reel into the lake. For the rest of the evening, Dad fished for his pole. He finally caught it and we all went home happy.

However many fish we caught we always buried them in my mother's flower garden. Dad said it would help her flowers grow. I think he just didn't want to clean them. For the most part, they were all rock bass and sun fish and very small. It was probably a smart move on his part.

One time when we were all finished fishing, we turned around to get the fish we had caught just in time to see a family of racoons running into the woods with our catch.

My father's favorite was always brook trout. When he worked near a lake, he would drop a line in the water in the morning and check it on his break. Whether he cooked them at home or over an open fire it was alway the same procedure.

Bill Pulling

MAIN DISH

Adirondack Recipe *Pan Fried Trout*

Fresh Trout	butter
salt & pepper	milk
flour	egg

Clean fish. Put some flour in a shallow dish. Sprinkle with salt and pepper. Mix milk and egg in shallow dish. Dip fish in milk mixture, dredge in flour mixture. Melt butter in cast iron frying pan until bubbling. Fry fish 5 minutes on each side until golden brown.

Salads, Sides & So On

Salads, Sides & So On

When you cook over an open fire only part of the meal gets done. You also need wonderful side dishes to finish off the meal. Potato salad is a staple at most every picnic. At my house we have several ways to make it. If my son Jamie is coming to dinner, it has to be Smooshie Potato Salad. One time I invited him for a picnic and there was no smooshie potato salad. Believe me, I never made that mistake again.

I learned to make it in Texas when I was first married. It has become a favorite with all my friends. The best part is you start with mashed potatoes so it is quick to make.

Nathan & Jamie Best chillaxin.

 ### SIDE DISH

Adirondack Recipe *Smooshie Potato Salad*

2 cups instant potato flakes	1/4 cup prepared yellow
2 cups boiling water	mustard (or enough to make
1/4 cup dill pickle juice	it sufficiently yellow)
1 cup Miracle Whip (NOT mayo)	1/2 cup chopped dill
4 hard boiled eggs, chopped	pickles

Mix potato flakes and water. Mixture will be quite stiff. Add pickle juice, Miracle Whip, and mustard. Mix well. Fold in eggs and pickles. Add salt and pepper to taste. Chill before serving.

Grandpa Best, my father-in-law Roger, makes the best normal potato salad I have ever had. I have to admit that sometimes he goes crazy with the onions but he always cuts them big enough so you can easily pick them out.

At all the Charbonneau Family Reunions, my cousins always flocked to my table. I may not have been the best cook, but I never put onions in my salads! That is just the way they liked it.

Roger Best

🌲 SIDE DISH

Adirondack Recipe   *Potato Salad*

4 lbs. potatoes cooked skinned and diced	5 hard boiled eggs, chopped
	1 cup mayonnaise
1 cup chopped sweet pickles	salt and pepper to taste
1 cup chopped dill pickles	some dill pickle juice for
1 big onion diced	taste not so much it is runny

Mix all ingredients together in large bowl. Salad is best if refrigerated over night.

When Roger gave me the recipe, he used terms like "a good amount." I put measurements as best as I could.

When my mother, Betty Pulling, made potato salad she left out the mustard and pickles and put in cucumbers and fresh tomatoes. You really had to eat it all the first day. The tomatoes weep if it is left overnight.

If you want to really impress the crowd, make Loaded Potato Salad. It is my daughter Scottie's recipe. She made it for a pot luck at church one time and I think I saw a group of men licking the bowl. It is that good.

Betty Pulling

 ## SIDE DISH

Adirondack Recipe   *Loaded Potato Salad*

3 lbs boiling potatoes	2 cups shredded cheddar
5-6 ribs celery, diced	cheese
1 cup chopped scallions	2 cups mayo
1 cup bacon bits	1/2 tsp black pepper

Cut potatoes into one inch cubes. Bring to a boil in heavily salted water. Reduce heat, simmer until potatoes are fork-tender, about 12 minutes. Drain and run under cold water. Mix all ingredients, taste and add salt if needed. As salad sits the potatoes will soak up a lot of the mayo. Don't panic, but you may need to add more!

Another salad my daughter Scottie invented is Chicken BLT Pasta Salad. It came about in the kitchen of a restaurant she was working in. She was bored and all the ingredients were there. The rest, as they say, is delicious history.

Scottie Best Glitz

SIDE DISH

Adirondack Recipe   *Chicken BLT Pasta Salad*

1 lb cellentani pasta, or smaller	2 cucumbers, diced, seeds removed
1 1/2 to 2 lbs chicken breast	2 packets ranch dressing mix
1 cup bacon bits	2 cups mayo
2 pints grape tomatoes, halved	2 cups buttermilk

Combine dressing mix, mayo and buttermilk. Set aside in refrigerator. Boil pasta in salted water for 10 minutes. Drain and cool under cold running water. Season chicken with salt and pepper, grill and dice. Combine dressing, pasta, chicken, bacon, and veggies. Chill at least 2 hours or overnight.

Scottie makes a great coleslaw too. She first started making it at the Pied Piper and since then she has perfected it. She nevers stops inventing new recipes or at least new ways to do the old ones.

One day she asked me if it was wrong to want to invite all her friends over and cook them delicious food. I told her it was fine... and when did she want me to come over!

SIDE DISH

Adirondack Recipe   Coleslaw

1 large head cabbage (or equivalent of preshredded)	super fine sugar (NOT powdered sugar)
1 cup shredded carrots	salt
mayo	pepper
white vinegar	celery seed

If starting with whole heads of cabbage; Remove and discard any outer leaves that show signs of wilting, dirt, etc. Finely shred cabbage by hand or in a food processor. Place cabbage and carrots in a large non-reactive container. Mix vinegar and sugar in a separate bowl until sugar dissolves. Add mayo, stir until smooth. The amount of dressing depends on several things like how big the head of cabbage is, and if you like your slaw lightly or heavily dressed. Use a ratio of 1 part sugar, 1 part vinegar, and 2 parts mayo. Add salt, pepper, and celery seed (to taste) to the dressing mixture. Keep in mind you can always add more seasoning, but you can't take it out! Pour dressing over cabbage and mix well. Taste and add more seasoning if needed. Let slaw sit, refrigerated, for a few hours. The cabbage will soften and the dressing will become thinner. Slaw can be eaten right away, but it's better the next day!

I learned to make Taco Salad from my mother-in-law, Doris Best. Somewhere along the line she started calling it Fiesta Salad, but either way it is a great salad.

I know people who will come to a picnic at my house based on this salad alone. It is a favorite among adults and kids alike.

Doris Best

 SIDE DISH

Adirondack Recipe *Taco Salad (aka Fiesta Salad)*

In a large bowl toss together:

chopped lettuce & tomatoes

shredded cheddar cheese

drained, canned kidney beans

crushed corn chips (Fritos)

Catalina dressing

Make as little, or as much as you want, but EAT IT IMMEDI-ATELY! It is not delicious once the chips get soggy. If traveling with this salad, mix lettuce, tomatoes, and beans. Add cheese, chips and dressing directly before serving.

My daughter Kelly is a big fan of pasta. She makes tortellini salad. She first had it at Berry College in Rome, Georgia. She figured out how to make it and now it is her father's favorite. He rarely cooks or makes anything but he will make this salad at the drop of a hat.

Kelly cooks and bakes all the time. Her daughters like to cook, too. They started with an easy bake oven and have graduated to the real thing.

Kelly Best

SIDE DISH

Adirondack Recipe   _Tortellini Salad_

1 pkg frozen cheese   _1-2 tomatoes depending on size_
  tortellini   _1/2 bottle Italian dressing_
1 can black olives

Boil tortellini in salted water according to package directions. Drain and run under cold water until pasta is cool. Drain olives and cut them in half. Chop tomatoes. Mix all ingredients with dressing. Salad should chill at least an hour before eating, but it's better the longer it sits. Optional additions include: Artichokes, Red onions, Cucumbers, Cubed cheese like provolone or swiss.

My husband, Yogi, does not like to cook. He would rather order out if I am not there to make him dinner. But there is one salad he will make any time he gets the chance. It is pea salad. It's another Texas thing and none of my kids will eat it.

He makes it with canned peas and my kids all hate canned peas. Sometimes when I make it I use frozen peas and it is better. I like it, although it is not my favorite. It is quick and easy to make.

Yogi & Jamie Best

SIDE DISH

Adirondack Recipe   *Pea Salad*

1 can peas   *1/2 cup mayo or Miracle Whip*
or equal amount frozen peas   salt & pepper
1/2 cup grated cheese
Place all ingredients in bowl, mix. Better if chilled for an hour. Optional chopped onions or chopped hard boiled eggs.

SIDE DISH

Adirondack Recipe   *Pasta Salad*

1 lb rotini pasta	1 bag frozen mixed veggies
1- 1 1/2 lbs grilled	(no need to thaw)
chicken breast, diced	1 can chick peas, drained
1 can kidney beans, drained	1 bottle Italian dressing

Cook pasta for 8-10 minutes in boiling heavily salted water. Drain pasta. Toss with remaining ingredients. Do not cool pasta first as hot pasta will absorb the flavor of the dressing better. Chill for 1-2 hours. Salad can be made vegetarian by omitting chicken.

SIDE DISH

Adirondack Recipe   *BBQ Baked Beans*

1 large can Grandma Brown	1/2 cup brown sugar
baked beans	1 cup prepared BBQ sauce
1 onion	1/4 cup ketchup
1/2 lb bacon	1 tbsp prepared yellow mustard

Chop bacon and sautee until crispy, drain. Reserve 2 tbsp bacon drippings. Dice onion and sautee in reserved drippings until translucent. Add sugar, BBQ sauce, ketchup, and mustard to onions. Cook stirring until sugar is dissolved and mixture is thick and bubbly. Stir together beans, onion mixture, and bacon. Bake for 20-30 minutes at 350. This recipe can be made in a dutch oven over a campfire.

Three of my uncles: Bill, George and Tom Charbonneau

SIDE DISH

Adirondack Recipe   *Bean Salad (aka 3 Bean Salad)*

Open several cans of beans:	chick peas
Italian green beans	lima beans
yellow wax beans	black beans
kidney beans	any bean you like

Open cans of beans, drain, put in large bowl. Cover with 2 parts vinegar to 1 part oil. Salt and pepper to taste. Cover and put in refrigerator for at least 3 hours. Best if served next day. Optional: chopped onion and chopped celery.

SIDE DISH

Adirondack Recipe   _Zesty Maccaroni Salad_

2 cups small pasta like shells, elbows, or (my favorite) ditalini

1 5-6oz jar sliced green olives with pimentos

4 ribs celery, diced   Black pepper to taste

1 1/2 cups Miracle Whip (NOT mayo)

1-2 tomatoes depending on size   1/2 bottle Italian dressing

Boil pasta in heavily salted water for 8-10 minutes. Drain and run under cold water until cool. Mix pasta, celery, olives (liquid and all), dressing and Miracle Whip. Add pepper to taste (salad will most likely be salty enough from the olives but add some if you like) Chill at least 1 hour. Dressing will be thin, but the pasta will absorb the liquid as it chills.

You can leave the Italian dressing out of the Zesty Maccaroni Salad and put in hard boiled eggs and tuna or shrimp and you have another salad.

SIDE DISH

Adirondack Recipe   _Cucumber Salad_

cucumbers   vinegar

vegetable oil   salt & pepper

Peel cucumbers and slice. Put in bowl. Cover with one part vinegar and two parts oil. Salt & pepper to taste. Cover and put in refrigerator overnight. Chopped onions optional.

SIDE DISH

Adirondack Recipe   *Grilled Cabbage*

1 head cabbage	1/2 tsp garlic powder
4 tsp butter	1/4 tsp pepper
4 slices bacon	2 tbsp grated Parmesan
1 tsp salt	cheese

Cut cabbage into four wedges. Place each wedge on a piece of doubled heavy-duty aluminum foil. Spread cut sides with butter. Mix spices together in a small container and sprinkle all of the mixture equally over each wedge. Wrap bacon around each wedge. Fold foil around cabbage, sealing each wedge tightly. Grill cabbage, covered, over medium heat for 40 minutes or until the cabbage is tender, turning twice.

Peggy, from left, Nancy, Pepper, Bobby and Edie, in front, Pulling on Edie's second birthday.

My mother used to make a couple of salads just for my father. He took his lunch to work everyday. He liked to take several sandwiches and some salad. He got up very early and had lunch at about 10 a.m. Then a second lunch at about 1 p.m. I only know because sometimes he would let me go to work with him.

Nancy & Bill Pulling at Broadacres Hospital in Utica Easter 1954. I was recovering from TB.

SIDE DISH

Adirondack Recipe   *Beet Salad*

1 can beets (chopped)	*1/2 cup mayo or Miracle Whip*
1/2 cup chopped onions	*salt & pepper*

Place all ingredients in bowl, mix. Better if chilled for an hour.

SIDE DISH

Adirondack Recipe   *Cottage Cheese Salad*

1 pint cottage cheese	*1/2 cup chopped*
salt & pepper	*green peppers*

Place all ingredients in bowl, mix.
Better if chilled for an hour.

Jane Nelson Tormey

It seems like I have known Jane Nelson forever. She was raised in Inlet. Her parents owned Nelson's Cottages right on 4th Lake. She graduated a year after me from the Town of Webb. Her dad managed McCauley Mountain and her mom was a teacher.

When I was a teenager, I was walking home in the pouring rain one day. A car pulled up beside me and a young man asked if I wanted a ride. Of course I said no. He persisted and every time I said no. All at once he stopped his car and got out. He said, "Nancy it's Kenny Nelson, I just wanted to give you a ride home."

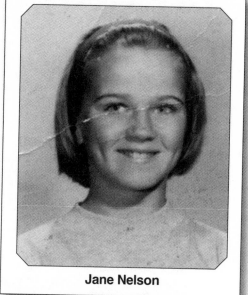

Jane Nelson

I was so embarrassed. I had known Jane's brother as long as I had known her. I got in the car and we both laughed.

Jane and I are friends on facebook and she keeps me informed on what's going on back in Old Forge. She works at the school so she knows everything!

Shortly after I started this book she made a post about Cooler Corn. It sounded so good that I couldn't leave it out.

When you are cooking outdoors and don't have lots of burners, it is a good thing when you can find a quick way to cook.

You take a clean cooler and fill it with shucked ears of corn. Pour boiling water over the corn until it is covered, close the top and wait.

In 30 minutes the corn will be perfectly cooked. The corn will remain at the perfect level of doneness for a couple of hours.

Learning To Cook
ADIRONDACK

BY NANCY PULLING BEST

Anna
The Spider

Written by Nancy Pulling Best
Illustrated by Mathew S. Capron

Published by NDI Publishing
2985 Powell Road, Blossvale NY 13308
www.nancydidit.com • 315.533.0816